THIS IS A PARRAGON BOOK

© Parragon 1996

Parragon
13-17 Avonbridge Trading Estate
Atlantic Road, Avonmouth,
Bristol, BS11 9QD

Produced by The Templar Company plc,
Pippbrook Mill, London Road, Dorking
Surrey RH4 1JE

Designed by Mark Kingsley Monks

Printed and bound in Great Britain

ISBN 0 75252 063 6

THE
Jam Pandas'
FIRST BOOK OF
Opposites

ILLUSTRATED BY STEPHANIE BOEY
WRITTEN BY CLAIRE STEEDEN

P

PARRAGON

The Jam Pandas are
very **happy**.
They are going to
the fair.

SAD

But the Marmalade Cat is **sad**, because he cannot go too.

When they get to
the fair, Pa pushes
the gate **open**.

OPEN

CLOSED

Ma pulls it **closed**.

TOP

BOTTOM

Peaches climbs up to the **top** of the helter-skelter, then whizzes down to the **bottom**.

At the merry-go-round
Pa rides on a **big** horse.

SMALL

Baby Jim Jam rides
on a **small** horse.

Peaches and Plum go on a ghost train. Outside it is **light**.

LIGHT

DARK

Inside it is **dark**
and scary!
They are both glad to
get off.

Pa drinks a **hot** cup of pear juice.

HOT

Ma eats a **cold** raspberry ice cream.

COLD

On the log ride Big Bamboo
sits at the back. Big Bamboo
gets **wet** and **dirty**, but Plum
stays **dry** and **clean**.

DIRTY
AND
WET

CLEAN
AND
DRY

EMPTY

SLOW

Some of the bumper cars
are **empty**, some are **full**.

They start off **slowly**,
then they go **fast**.

LONG
AND
THIN

Grandma likes to look at
the magic mirrors.
Some make
her look **long** and **thin**.

SHORT
AND
FAT

Others make her look
short and **fat**.

Soon it is time to go.
All the family are
wide **awake** except for
Baby Jim Jam.
He is fast **asleep**.

AWAKE

ASLEEP

The Jam Pandas leave the **noisy** fair. Soon they are all fast asleep in their **quiet** home.

QUIET

Titles in this series include: